Riding the Earthboy 40

ebook: #10.99

1/17/24

Riding the Earthboy 40

James Welch

Introduction by James Tate

PENGUIN POETS

for Lois

PENGUIN BOOKS
Published by the Penguin Group
Penguin Group (USA) Inc., 375 Hudson Street, New York, New York 10014, U.S.A.
Penguin Group (Canada), 10 Alcorn Avenue, Toronto, Ontario,
Canada M4V 3B2 (a division of Pearson Penguin Canada Inc.)
Penguin Books Ltd, 80 Strand, London WC2 0RL, England
Penguin Ireland, 25 St Stephen's Green, Dublin 2, Ireland (a division of Penguin Books Ltd)
Penguin Group (Australia), 250 Camberwell Road, Camberwell,
Victoria 3124, Australia (a division of Pearson Australia Group Pty Ltd)
Penguin Books India Pvt Ltd, 11 Community Centre, Panchsheel Park, New Delhi – 110 017, India
Penguin Group (NZ), cnr Airborne and Rosedale Roads, Albany,
Auckland, New Zealand (a division of Pearson New Zealand Ltd)
Penguin Books (South Africa) (Pty) Ltd, 24 Sturdee Avenue, Rosebank, Johannesburg 2196, South Africa

Penguin Books Ltd, Registered Offices:
80 Strand, London WC2R 0RL, England

First published in the United States of America by Confluence Press 1990
This edition with an introduction by James Tate published in Penguin Books 2004

1 3 5 7 9 10 8 6 4 2

CIP data available
ISBN 0 14 30.3439 1

Printed in the United States of America

Contents

Hugo divided his collections like this too.

KNIVES

THE RENEGADE WANTS WORDS

Introduction

James Welch's first and only book of poems, *Riding the Earthboy 40*, has passed that most exacting of tests, Time. Thirty-three years have passed since its initial publication, and it reads as fresh and new as if it had been published yesterday. Its strong measured rhythms, recurrent imagery, and lyrical precision—all these qualities mix together to produce a book of poems so singular and timeless it is no wonder the book is being reissued now in a time when last year's books are already out of print. It is simply too beautiful to forget.

Given the consistency of the narrator's voice, the book reads almost as if it were one long poem. The speaker's love and constant regard for nature, even when it may precipitate his doom, is the prevailing spirit that runs through the book. The threat of death, or at the very least, destitution, is presented in the same stoic tone as an appreciation of a young girl's beauty. The general sadness may be that of a young man, but there is a wisdom here that seems to have been inherited from the earth.

There is hope, there is always hope. And that comes mostly in the belief in tradition, traditions that refuse to die even in the face of grim poverty and with exposure to corrupting influences.

Celebrate. The days are grim.

yeah, but come on how that almost feels sarcastic

These are the tensions struggling within the poems.

To stay alive this way, it's hard.

Moon, snakes, snow, horses, bars, hawks, all these and so much more come back to haunt us until a peculiar magic settles over the landscape again and again. Poverty is not the worst thing that can happen to a person. Loss of belief is. And throughout this book the speaker may be tempted by despair, but he never really succumbs, or at least not for long.

James Welch never returned to poetry after this moving first book. In

1974, Harper & Row published his first novel, *Winter in the Blood*, an instant classic that has remained in print ever since. Through the eyes of one intelligent young man we experience the reality of reservation life— the cattle-ranching, family, the binges, the women, the shattered heritage. It is the same world that occupies Welch's poetry, but the sustained plot and deeper characterizations allowed him to enlarge his story and fill in the thousands of details that would break our hearts. Welch needed the full canvas for the stories he was going to tell over the next thirty years. As much as I would like to imagine the poems he might have written, I will always be grateful for the books he did write. The very last, *The Heartsong of Charging Elk*, stands on the very top tier of American fiction ever written, and who can ask for more than that.

But poetry says things that nothing else can. It snares the edges of the unspeakable. It grazes dreams. It stands with feet in several worlds. It says two or three things at once, and then denies them all in favor of silence.

> *His sins were numerous, this wrong man.*
> *Buttes were good to listen from. With thunder-*
> *hands his father shaped the dust, circled*
> *fire, tumbled up the wind to make a fool.*
> *Now the fool is dead. His bones go back*
> *so scarred in time, the buttes are young to look*
> *for signs that say a man could love his fate,*
> *that winter in the blood is one sad thing.*

This is that magnificent dance of language that cannot be translated into prose. Each element is perfectly clear, and, yet, together they form a kind of kaleidoscope, rotating, moving, through endless possibilities. Only real poets can achieve this perfect balance. James Welch will always be one of those real poets.

Riding the Earthboy 40

KNIVES

Magic Fox

They shook the green leaves down,
those men that rattled
in their sleep. Truth became
a nightmare to their fox.
He turned their horses into fish,
or was it horses strung
like fish, or fish like fish
hung naked in the wind?

Stars fell upon their catch.
A girl, not yet twenty-four
but blonde as morning birds, began
a dance that drew the men in
green around her skirts.
In dust her magic jangled memories
of dawn, till fox and grief
turned nightmare in their sleep.

And this: fish not fish but stars
that fell into their dreams.

Verifying the Dead

We tore the green tree down
searching for my bones.
A coyote drove the day back
half a step until we killed
both him and it. Our knives
became a bed for quick things.
It's him all right
I heard old Nine Pipe say.
As we turned away,
a woman blue as night
stepped from my bundle,
rubbed her hips and sang
of a country like this far off.

hm. I do see some
struggle here with
the last line. He has
trouble leaving his poems...

Song for the Season

It was September,
September fourth I think
the night his light went out
in the great bedroom
on the lake. Moontime
seared the junipers
rimming the great house.

September and the mountain ash
was stopped quite cold,
its spindly bole going dead
as though the fingers
of the quite dead man
had pinched a vital nerve.

Think of it. The man had done
so much and now, even
the trees would fold
and wither at his icy touch.

His small boat, tied securely
to the dock, fiddled out
across the lake its dirge.

Too late, he found, that for the great
as well as for the weak,
the wrong instruments ease you out
and the coming on of autumn.

Dreaming Winter

Don't ask me if these knives are real.
I could paint a king or show a map
the way home—to go like this:
wobble me back to a tiger's dream,
a dream of knives and bones too common
to be exposed. My secrets are ignored.

Here comes the man I love. His coat is wet
and his face is falling like the leaves,
tobacco stains on his Polish teeth.
I could tell jokes about him—one up
for the man who brags a lot, laughs
a little and hangs his name on the nearest knob.
Don't ask me. I know it's only hunger.

I saw that king—the one my sister knew
but was allergic to. Her face ran until
his eyes became the white of several winters.
Snow on his bed told him that the silky tears
were uniformly mad and all the money in the world
couldn't bring him to a tragic end. Shame
or fortune tricked me to his table, shattered
my one standing lie with new kinds of fame.

Have mercy on me, Lord. Really. If I should die
before I wake, take me to that place I just heard
banging in my ears. Don't ask me. Let me join
the other kings, the ones who trade their knives
for a sack of keys. Let me open any door,
stand winter still and drown in a common dream.

Toward Dawn

Today I search for a name.
Not too long, they said,
nor short. A deer crashes
in the wood. A skunk
swaggers to the distant creek.
There is a moment, I think,
when the eyes speak
and speak of a world too much.
Such a moment, a life.

Blue Like Death

You see, the problem is
no more for the road. Moon fails
in snow between the moon
and you. Your eyes ignite
the way that butterfly
should move had you not killed it
in a dream of love.

The road forked back
and will fork again the day
you earn your lies,
the thrill of being what you are
when shacks begin to move
and coyotes kill the snakes
you keep safe at home in jars.

The girl let you out. She prized
your going the way some people
help a drunk to fall.
Easy does it, one two three
and let him lie. For he was blue
and dirt is where the bones
meet. You met his eyes

out there where the road dips
and children whipped the snake
you called Frank to death
with sticks. Now you understand:
the way is not your going
but an end. That road awaits
the moon that falls between
the snow and you, your stalking home.

8

Crystal

Near Canada, between patches
of spring wheat and tumbleweed,
the horses begin to sing.
Why should I, drunk
as I am, try to understand?
Here, there, the moon blooms,
draws a bead on coyotes
abroad, afraid to lie down,
golden in Crystal's gray dawn.

Picnic Weather

I know the songs we sang,
the old routine, the dozen masks
you painted when we left you
alone, afraid, frightened of yourself
the day the bull snakes rose,
seething out of dreams, has made you
what you are—alone, afraid, stronger.

Here we go again. The same sad tune.
You knew you would die some night,
alone, no folks, and I, no face, alone,
weaker in the knees and in the heart.
Picture this as your epitaph:
The bull snakes rising against you,
you popping their necks with a clean jerk
and the sky the drab blue of spring.

Winter now: here your image dies.
I can't grab hold of you like the snakes.
I know the dream: you, alone, stronger
than the night I popped your neck,
left you squirming on the ground, afraid
you'd find your hole and disappear,
and me, my fingers strong around your head,
my head making clicking sounds—
nothing like the music in your bones.

Directions to the Nomad

Past the school and down
this little incline—
you can't miss it.
Tons of bricks and babies
blue from the waist down.
Their heads are cheese
and loll as though
bricks became their brains.

What's that—the noble savage?
He's around, spooked and colored
by the fish he eats,
red for rainbow, blue
for the moon. He instructs stars,
but only to the thinnest wolf.

When you get there
tell the mad decaying creep
we miss him. We never
meant it. He'll treat you right,
show you poems
the black bear couldn't dream.
One more thing—if he tries
to teach you mountains
or whisper imagined love
to the tamarack, tell him
you adore him,
then get the hell out, fast.

Gesture Down to Guatemala
(For Dave McElroy)

All things come cheap when schools turn civic
in despair. You bless the kids, gringo, rough shoes
banging past the comedor. Quick handout, one friend.

Here no one calls you sweetheart. Fried beans are foreign
and wind will toss your face in other fields—some dream.
Pantomimes are common; a pat stance, the best.

Always playing yourself up to second fiddle
and angry to learn, you left the pines to turn
a bad direction. Clouds and friends can mix you up.

Shawls color the rainbow a new odor. Those pajamas
you sport are simply tired old friends.
(Why do they have to paint the walls of houses pink?)

Drink too much or let the Indians touch you
with terrible words that mean you have chosen right
and that lovely blonde from Montana died a year ago

in Peru. (Paint is pink in Missoula too.) Before you teach
the clouds your past, or learn new names in Mayan ruins,
call me amigo, break old women down to gestures

of love, a quick *Pase adelante, jovencito, pase!*

Life Support System

Again I am in Gallup
and the wind grazes my face.
If I cross the street
I will surely be killed.

Men whisper in alleys.
A girl lifts her arms
to the window, crying
for a boy she loses
always this time of year.

My eyes kiss that hot wind.
I reach for her hair.
The men continue to whisper.
In time they will notice
what it has taken us moons
and just such alleys to decide.

The World's Only Corn Palace

They came with knives and sticks—
no one called, no one reminded
the wild man of his right to scream,
to fall sobbing to his knees.
With sticks they came—this pack
so bent on killing all his bones.

Some looked away; others in their throats
began to laugh, not loud, but blue,
a winter blue that followed
mongrels out the door. With knives
those killers carved initials on his heart
till his eyes grew white with wonder.

Thunderbird came heavy on our heads.
Too much of a good thing
can spoil it for poets, you said.
I agreed. Down by the river we sang
sad tunes and O the stars
were bright that melancholy night.

Arizona Highways

I see her seventeen,
a lady dark, turquoise
on her wrists. The land
astounded by a sweeping rain
becomes her skin. Clouds
begin to mend my broken eyes.

I see her singing by a broken shack,
eyes so black it must be dawn.
I hum along, act sober,
tell her I could love her
if she dressed better, if her father   *Ouch.*
got a job and beat her more.
Eulynda. There's a name   *heh.*
I could live with. I could
thrash away the nuns, tell them
I adopt this girl, dark,
seventeen, silver on her fingers,
in the name of the father, son,   *love it*
and me, the holy ghost.
Why not? Mormons do less
with less. Didn't her ancestors
live in cliffs, no plumbing,
just a lot of love and corn?
Me, that's corn, pollen
in her hair. East, south, west, north—
now I see my role—religious.

The Indian politician made her laugh.
Her silver jingled in her throat,
those songs, her fingers busy
on his sleeve. Fathers, forgive me.
She knows me in her Tchindii dream,
always a little pale, too much
bourbon in my nose, my shoes
too clean, belly soft as hers.

I'll move on. My schedule
says Many Farms tomorrow, then
on to Window Rock, and finally home,
that weathered nude, distant
as the cloud I came in on.

Night Hawk

He's worried about his rights.
They are clear: the air.
Night holds just one secret.
He doesn't know it
so he cries air, the air.

I know finicky secrets.
In the mountains, for instance,
a man lives close to his eyes.
For another, he speaks
with his hands. And another:
man is afraid of his dark.

Trestles by the Blackfoot

Fools by chance, we traveled
cavalier toward death. Fish ran up
to break the black pools
we could not reach. Evening
and the rattle train shook trestles
one quiet inch behind our eyes.

Why not this sentimental stance?
You, me, the shaggy manes
we chose to disappear, inky caps
so spurious we clapped
our hands for calm. You see
the danger in your pose? One foot
between the ties, the other
in your mouth? Inky does

as inky do. It just won't do.
Funky jokes can't separate
this monster from his meal.
Let's be nice, pretend we sail
twelve feet out and down,

perfect cats returning from their night,
sunrise, knives between
their teeth, lies as clean as foam
we leave behind our toes.
Sliced and faded, those fish
will know us by the noise we chose—
black train rattle, steel on steel.

THE RENEGADE
WANTS WORDS

In My First Hard Springtime

Those red men you offended were my brothers.
Town drinkers, Buckles Pipe, Star Boy,
Billy Fox, were blood to bison. Albert Heavy Runner
was never civic. You are white and common.

Record trout in Willow Creek chose me
to deify. My horse, Centaur, part cayuse,
was fast and mad and black. Dandy in flat hat
and buckskin, I rode the town and called it mine.

A slow hot wind tumbled dust against my door.
Fed and fair, you mocked my philosophic nose,
my badger hair. I rolled your deference
in the hay and named it love and lasting.

Starved to visions, famous cronies top Mount Chief
for names to give respect to Blackfeet streets.
I could deny them in my first hard springtime,
but choose amazed to ride you down with hunger.

Christmas Comes to Moccasin Flat

Christmas comes like this: Wise men
unhurried, candles bought on credit (poor price
for calves), warriors face down in wine sleep.
Winds cheat to pull heat from smoke.

Friends sit in chinked cabins, stare out
plastic windows and wait for commodities.
Charlie Blackbird, twenty miles from church
and bar, stabs his fire with flint.

When drunks drain radiators for love
or need, chiefs eat snow and talk of change,
an urge to laugh pounding their ribs.
Elk play games in high country.

Medicine Woman, clay pipe and twist tobacco,
calls each blizzard by name and predicts
five o'clock by spitting at her television.
Children lean into her breath to beg a story:

Something about honor and passion,
warriors back with meat and song,
a peculiar evening star, quick vision of birth.
Blackbird feeds his fire. Outside, a quick 30 below.

In My Lifetime

This day the children of Speakthunder
run the wrong man, a saint unable
to love a weasel way, able only to smile
and drink the wind that makes the others go.
Trees are ancient in his breath.
His bleeding feet tell a story of run
the sacred way, chase the antelope naked
till it drops, the odor of run
quiet in his blood. He watches cactus
jump against the moon. Moon is speaking
woman to the ancient fire. Always woman.

His sins were numerous, this wrong man.
Buttes were good to listen from. With thunder-
hands his father shaped the dust, circled
fire, tumbled up the wind to make a fool.
Now the fool is dead. His bones go back
so scarred in time, the buttes are young to look
for signs that say a man could love his fate,
that winter in the blood is one sad thing.

Such a drop. So depressing. And creepy!

His sins—I don't explain. Desperate in my song,
I run these woman hills, translate wind
to mean a kind of life, the children of Speakthunder
are never wrong and I am rhythm to strong medicine.

So powerful!

Spring for All Seasons

Let the sloughs back up and history
will claim that lakes were here
and Indians poled their way from Asia
past monsoons and puddled heat of carp.
We know better. We know this land
wouldn't bring a dime for rain in China.

Practice your grin when clouds are red,
sky falls blue against the buttes.
Morning brings flood to verbena, planted
by some fool who thinks July forgets
the past. Our past is ritual,
cattle marching one way to remembered mud.

Bring on the fools. Let some sap declare
a ten year rain, a Japanese current
to carry us west to rain forests or east
or south and down. Eskimos are planting
corn where lunar waves crawl the ice,
snow, the Arctic desert gone.

There Are Silent Legends

You might be bucking bales or hazing strays
and get a bug in your ear, some meaningless
tapping on the wind. You'd look up,
relax your stare until you saw a willow shift
or a hasty pheasant flushed. He'd be there,
watching your eyes jump to the black hair hung
against the ditch bank. Deafy knew he was a legend,
could see it in your face. Drunk, just enough beard,
a mad Mongol sniffing a few feet ahead
of your downwind fear. Dusk and birdsongs
banged against his drum-tight ear and you could yell
until his thin body turned to stone.

Though he never heard your stories, never heard the one
you told about the crazy Indian, the slick black hair
dangling at his belt, his ears lost mysterious
in St. Louis in that alley no one quite recalls—
Though wind has shut his ears for good, he squats
for hours at the slough, skipping stones, dreaming
of a moon, the quiet nights and a not quite done
love with a lady high in costly red shoes.

Harlem, Montana: Just Off the Reservation

We need no runners here. Booze is law
and all the Indians drink in the best tavern.
Money is free if you're poor enough.
Disgusted, busted whites are running
for office in this town. The constable,
a local farmer, plants the jail with wild
raven-haired stiffs who beg just one more drink.
One drunk, a former Methodist, becomes a saint
in the Indian church, bugs the plaster man
on the cross with snakes. If his knuckles broke,
he'd see those women wail the graves goodbye.

Goodbye, goodbye, Harlem on the rocks,
so bigoted, you forget the latest joke,
so lonely, you'd welcome a battalion of Turks
to rule your women. What you don't know,
what you will never know or want to learn—
Turks aren't white. Turks are olive, unwelcome
alive in any town. Turks would use
your one dingy park to declare a need for loot.
Turks say bring it, step quickly, lay down and dead.

Here we are when men were nice. This photo, hung
in the New England Hotel lobby, shows them nicer
than pie, agreeable to the warring bands of redskins
who demanded protection money for the price of food.
Now, only Hutterites out north are nice. We hate
them. They are tough and their crops are always good.
We accuse them of idiocy and believe their belief all wrong.

Harlem, your hotel is overnamed, your children
are raggedy-assed but you go on, survive
the bad food from the two cafes and peddle
your hate for the wild who bring you money.
When you die, if you die, will you remember
the three young bucks who shot the grocery up,
locked themselves in and cried for days, we're rich,
help us, oh God, we're rich.

Riding the Earthboy 40

Earthboy: so simple his name
should ring a bell for sinners.
Beneath the clowny hat, his eyes
so shot the children called him
dirt, Earthboy farmed this land
and farmed the sky with words.

The dirt is dead. Gone to seed
his rows become marker to a grave
vast as anything but dirt.
Bones should never tell a story
to a bad beginner. I ride
romantic to those words,

those foolish claims that he
was better than dirt, or rain
that bleached his cabin
white as bone. Scattered in the wind
Earthboy calls me from my dream:
Dirt is where the dreams must end.

hm. 18 lines. This feels like a Roethke exercise

Going to Remake This World

Morning and the snow might fall forever.
I keep busy. I watch the yellow dogs
chase creeping cars filled with Indians
on their way to the tribal office.
Grateful trees tickle the busy underside
of our snow-fat sky. My mind is right,
I think, and you will come today
for sure, this day when the snow falls.

From my window, I see bundled Doris Horseman,
black in the blowing snow, her raving son,
Horace, too busy counting flakes to hide his face.
He doesn't know. He kicks my dog
and glares at me, too dumb to thank the men
who keep him on relief and his mama drunk.

My radio reminds me that Hawaii calls
every afternoon at two. Moose Jaw is overcast,
twelve below and blowing. Some people . . .
Listen: if you do not come this day, today
of all days, there is another time
when breeze is tropic and riffs the green sap
forever up these crooked cottonwoods. Sometimes,
you know, the snow never falls forever.

Plea to Those Who Matter

You don't know I pretend my dumb.
My songs often wise, my bells could chase
the snow across these whistle-black plains.
Celebrate. The days are grim. Call your winds
to blast these bundled streets and patronize
my past of poverty and 4-day feasts.

Don't ignore me. I'll build my face a different way,
a way to make you know that I am no longer
proud, my name not strong enough to stand alone.
If I lie and say you took me for a friend,
patched together in my thin bones,
will you help me be cunning and noisy as the wind?

I have plans to burn my drum, move out
and civilize this hair. See my nose? I smash it
straight for you. These teeth? I scrub my teeth
away with stones. I know you help me now I matter.
And I—I come to you, head down, bleeding from my smile,
happy for the snow clean hands of you, my friends.

ugh. So damn
Sardonic

This is not
a happy poem

The Man from Washington

The end came easy for most of us.
Packed away in our crude beginnings
in some far corner of a flat world,
we didn't expect much more
than firewood and buffalo robes
to keep us warm. The man came down,
a slouching dwarf with rainwater eyes,
and spoke to us. He promised
that life would go on as usual,
that treaties would be signed, and everyone—
man, woman and child—would be inoculated
against a world in which we had no part,
a world of money, promise and disease.

Blackfeet, Blood and Piegan Hunters

If we raced a century over hills
that ended years before, people couldn't
say our run was simply poverty or promise
for a better end. We ended sometime
back in recollections of glory, myths
that meant the hunters meant a lot
to starving wives and bad painters. *heh. ouch.*

Let glory go the way of all sad things.
Children need a myth that tells them be alive,
forget the hair that made you Blood, the blood
the buffalo left, once for meat, before
other hunters gifted land with lead for hides.

Comfortable we drink and string together stories
of white buffalo, medicine men who promised
and delivered horrible cures for hunger,
lovely tales of war and white men massacres.
Meaning gone, we dance for pennies now,
our feet jangling dust that hides the bones
of sainted Indians. Look away and we are gone.
Look back. Tracks are there, a little faint,
our song strong enough for headstrong hunters
who look ahead to one more kill.

The Last Priest Didn't Even Say Goodbye

The wages of sin is to live where
the mountains give down to the Indian town.
Even the priest has decorated the one pink church
with hate and hate for sweat.
I planned a celebration, hard candy
for the kids, more hate for the old.
The priest wasn't in. His study smelled
of incense and bourbon. The saints all disapproved.
The Virgin glared down and said the priest is gone.

The local jokers say he lasted longer than most.
The graveyard is empty, the women live forever
 and the kids . ✗) comma
the kids are fishing for the priest's black hat. ugh.
                                              so dark.

D-Y Bar

The tune is cowboy; the words, sentimental crap.
Farther out, wind is mending sagebrush,
stapling it to earth in rows only a badger
would recommend. Reservoirs are dry,
the sky commands a cloud high
to skip the Breaks bristling with heat
and stunted pine.

In stunted light, Bear Child tells a story
to the mirror. He acts his name out,
creeks muscling gorges fill his glass
with gumbo. The bear crawls on all fours
and barks like a dog. Slithering snake-wise
he balances a nickel on his nose. The effect,
a snake in heat.

We all know our names here. Summer is a poor
season to skip this place or complain
about marauding snakes. Often when wind
is cool off mountains and the flats
are green, cars stop for gas, motors clicking
warm to songs of a junction bar, head down,
the dormant bear.

The Only Bar in Dixon

These Indians once imitated life.
Whatever made them warm
they called wine, song or sleep,
a lucky number on the tribal roll.

Now the stores have gone the gray
of this November sky. Cars
whistle by, chrome wind, knowing
something lethal in the dust.

A man could build a reputation here.
Take that redhead at the bar—
She knows we're thugs, killers
on a fishing trip with luck.

No luck. No room for those
sensitive enough to know they're beat. *Ouch. Such a drop.*
Even the Flathead turns away,
a river thick with bodies,

Indians on their way to Canada.
Take the redhead—yours for just a word,
a promise that the wind will warm
and all the saints come back for laughs.

Thanksgiving at Snake Butte

In time we rode that trail
up the butte as far as time
would let us. The answer to our time
lay hidden in the long grasses
on the top. Antelope scattered

through the rocks before us, clattered
unseen down the easy slope to the west.
Our horses balked, stiff-legged,
their nostrils flared at something unseen
gliding smoothly through brush away.

On top, our horses broke, loped through
a small stand of stunted pine, then jolted
to a nervous walk. Before us lay
the smooth stones of our ancestors, the fish,
the lizard, snake and bent-kneed

bowman—etched by something crude,
by a wandering race, driven by their names
for time: its winds, its rain, its snow
and the cold moon tugging at the crude figures
in this, the season of their loss.

hm. Not te strongest
ending he could have
landed on . . .

The Renegade Wants Words

We died in Zortman on a Sunday
in the square, beneath sky so blue
the eagles spoke in foreign tongues.
Our deeds were numbered: burning homes,
stealing women, wine and gold.

No one spoke of our good side,
those times we fed the hulking idiot,
mapped these plains with sticks
and flint, drove herds of bison wild
for meat and legend. We expected

no gratitude, no mercy on our heads.
But a word—the way we rode
naked across these burning hills.
Perhaps spring breakup made us move
and trust in stars. Ice, not will,

made our women ice. We burned
homes for heat. painted our bodies
in blood. Who can talk revenge?
Were we wild for wanting men to listen
to the earth, to plant only by moons?

In Zortman on a Sunday we died.
No bells, no man in black
to tell us where we failed.
Makeshift hangman, our necks,
noon and the eagles—not one good word.

Ugh. His world is so viscious. I'm really curious to know more about him...

DAY AFTER
CHASING PORCUPINES

Day After Chasing Porcupines

Rain came. Fog out of the slough and horses
asleep in the barn. In the field, sparrow hawks
glittered through the morning clouds.

No dreamers knew the rain. Wind ruffled quills
in the mongrel's nose. He sighed cautiously,
kicked further beneath the weathered shed and slept.

Timid chickens watched chickens in the puddles.
Watching the chickens, yellow eyes harsh
below the wind-drifting clouds, sparrow hawks.

Horses stamped in the barn. The mongrel whimpered
in his dream, wind ruffled his mongrel tail,
the lazy cattails and the rain.

Surviving

The day-long cold hard rain drove
like sun through all the cedar sky
we had that late fall. We huddled
close as cows before the bellied stove.
Told stories. Blackbird cleared his mind,
thought of things he'd left behind, spoke:

"Oftentimes, when sun was easy in my bones,
I dreamed of ways to make this land."
We envied eagles easy in their range.
"That thin girl, old cook's kid, stripped naked
for a coke or two and cooked her special stew
round back of the mess tent Sundays."
Sparrows skittered through the black brush.

That night the moon slipped a notch, hung
black for just a second, just long enough
for wet black things to sneak away our cache
of meat. To stay alive this way, it's hard. . . .

Snow Country Weavers

A time to tell you things are well.
Birds flew south a year ago.
One returned, a blue-wing teal
wild with news of his mother's love.

Mention me to friends. Say
Wolves are dying at my door,
the winter drives them from their meat.
Say this: say in my mind

I saw your spiders weaving threads
to bandage up the day. And more,
those webs were filled with words
that tumbled meaning into wind.

Visit

I come alone. To surprise you
I leave no sign, my name
shucked at the familiar gate.

Your name is implied in exile.
I bring meat for your memory,
wine for the skinning of muskrats.

I leave this wood, not much,
but enough to streak your face
a winter red despair.

Why no songs, no ceremony?
Set your traps to catch my one
last track, the peculiar scent,

goodbyes creaking in the pines.

Dancing Man

He swung gracefully into midnight
that man on the plains.
The stories he told were true enough
and we were young
to understand his beetle eye.
It wasn't till later
the dream broke
and we spun solid as a rock
back to the cold cactus ground,
winehappy and stubborn.

All it takes: a few sticks,
a fire, all the tea
in China . . .

there isn't much to do
nights
Heart Butte
in the dead of spring.

Birth on Range 18

His great thighs nosed the pebbles;
his head rolled in the socket

of the earth; he became the sky
with one quick jerk. The green of spring

came hard and the mother, bearing
easy, one two three, caught our stare

and stared our eyes away. Moon
eclipsed the night. We rode the wind

the only distance we could muster—
quick paces and a space of mind.

The Wrath of Lester Lame Bull

Bears are in the cabbage again,
cunning soles crashing down carrots,
faces thick to wear a turnip green.
Not even the onion dissents.

Lester Lame Bull in his garden grows
twenty rows of winter store,
a piddling score to court
against the blue of mountain ash.

Cottonwood limbs rattle his bones.
Lester storms those pesky winds,
stoning crows from purple cups.
Quirky grins are thick in muscatel.

Elephants are whispering in backyards.

There is a Right Way

The justice of the prairie hawk
moved me; his wings tipped
the wind just right and the mouse
was any mouse. I came away,
broken from my standing spot,
dizzy with the sense of a world
trying to be right, and the mouse
a part of a wind that stirs the plains.

Getting Things Straight

Is the sun the same drab gold?
The hawk—is he still rising, circling,
falling above the field? And the rolling day,
it will never stop? It means nothing?
Will it end the way history ended when
the last giant climbed Heart Butte, had his vision,
came back to town and drank himself
sick? The hawk has spotted a mouse.
Wheeling, falling, stumbling to a stop,
he watches the snake ribbon quickly
under a rock. What does it mean?
He flashes his wings to the sun, bobs
twice and lifts, screaming
off the ground. Does it mean this to him:
the mouse, a snake, the dozen angry days
still rolling since his last good feed?
Who offers him a friendly meal?
Am I strangling in his grip?
Is he my vision?

Ugh

*I ᴅᴠᴜ
ɪ t.
500 good*

The Versatile Historian

I came through autumn forests needing
wind that needed fire. Sun on larch,
fir, the ponderosa told me to forget
the friends I needed years ago.
Sky is all the rage in country steeped
in lore, the troubled Indians wise within
their graves. The chanting clouds
crowded against the lowest peak. I sang
of trouble to the north. Sleeping weasels robbed
my song of real words. Everywhere, rhythm raged.
Sun beneath my feet, I became
the statue needing friends in wind
that needed fire, mountains to bang against.

THE DAY
THE CHILDREN
TOOK OVER

The Day the Children Took Over

And though the sky was bright, snow fell down.
Children ran out. Mothers read letters
that said the world would end in fire.
Snow fell on driveways, on trestles and trees.
It fell on lovers locked together
in bedrooms and back seats of new Buicks
out of sight in green wild fields.

And yes, it fell with a vengeance
on statesmen who predicted peace in our time.
Priests who left the pulpit for a fine new wife
walked about, pure and heavy beneath a wet sun.

All around town, children ran out,
rolled their snow, stuck buttons, carrots,
old hats and bits of coal on shapeless lumps
to create life, in their own image.

finally something positive

Call to Arms

We spoke like public saints
to the people assembled in the square.
Our gestures swayed the morning light
and bathed the town in public guilt.

All the weather poured down that hour
our lips witched the ears of thousands.
Whiny kids broke from their mother's arms,
charged the fields, armed with sticks.

Men wept and women clutched their steaming
heads and beat the savage mildness
from their hearts. The eyes were with us,
every one, and we were with the storm.

We rode out that night, our ponchos slick
and battered down against our thighs.
Our horses knew the way. None looked behind,
but heard the mindless suck of savage booted feet.

Two for the Festival

No sun but awkward rhymes the sun
arrested in its curve. A boy lit up
the night, his coattails flying
in electric flame. In town
the usual customer, one drink and home,
stone figure in the weeds, looked up
and saw his future falling.

I know this boy, a weak chinned Greek
drowning cats in clouds. One drink,
the customer and town drove bleeding
strangers sane. A boy lit up the road,
falling. Two dancers passed, one young,
the other awkward in his rhyme.
He carried in his hand a blind toad,

a fox and thirteen lumpy stones.
Money listened; all wars stood still
till the arc of a customer's past
reflected in his face. The rest is real:
black-faced, the boy fell smiling
through the weeds. A toad glistened
in the sky. Fox, the awkward dancer,
hugged his stones. One drink, then home.

[Handwritten annotation, right margin:] So lovely ... but so heavily stopped ... I almost want some long moment of relief, like a breath exhaled.

[Handwritten annotation, below poem:] Oh that's beautiful!

You Gone, the King Dead

The heater's click and hum, smoke
from a distant cabin in the woods,
a meadowlark—you have not come.

I accuse them of taking you, the members
of the wedding, to some careless feast
across the land, beyond an evening slough.

Snows come gently from the south.
Heavy, heavy the house creaks assassin,
heard only by the man who dies alone.

His hand is on my shoulder. Something in his touch
tells me he is wise and knows the drifting
snow will smother any love I try.

Silent at his side, the woman I take
to be his bride, lifts a finger to my brain,
signals I am dead. Snow blows gently

from the south. The man, not tall but wide
across the heart, beckons to his unfamiliar bride,
touches her hand and drifts, upward to the stars.

Day to Make Up Incompletes

Because the day came (and now,
why not, because I am older)
that people fell dropping
not hard or fast, but soft
like the cottonwood snow
in my mother's yard, and the soft grasses
of my father's fields swarmed
before a thickening wind
out of the north,
I came (why not) to the conclusion
of rain beating the shingle roof
above my bed, and this day
like all my days
found me badly in need
of encyclopedias
and moths to tickle the itch
from my burning feet.

Counting Clouds

A long way to come—
this rain so old my bones
crackle no before you speak.
A way to come: downwind
before the sudden clouds appear,
turn you statue—no, I say,
no to the north and no, no
to your crummy mirror.

Once I loved this gravy land
so famous in my blood
my hair turned black
with love. A way to think:
so cold the sun could call me
friend. Now the daughters
call me son till wheat
and sun work one against me.

(He was good, had friends.
Never knew the color
of his past, those days
the gentle fish
danced gentle to his arms.)

No, the dancing man could never
teach you sundown, or show
the way a river ends
in wine. I forget the way
the days go by, but it must
be easy—counting clouds
or drinking beer with friends.

Now you go the rhymes
grow silly in these bones.
The no dissolves itself
in tears, in rain, the acid rain
of lost daughters in Mexico.

hm.

Strong ending?

Grandma's Man

That day she threw the goose over the roof
of the cowshed, put her hand to her lips
and sucked, cursing, the world ended. In blood
her world ended though these past twenty years
have healed the bite and that silly goose
is preening in her favorite pillow.

Her husband was a fool. He laughed too long
at lies told by girls whose easy virtue disappeared
when he passed stumble-bum down the Sunday street.
Baled hay in his every forty, cows on his alloted range,
his quick sorrel quarter-horse, all neglected for
the palms of friends. Then, he began to paint LIFE.

His first attempt was all about a goose that bit
the hand that fed it. The obstacles were great.
Insurmountable. His fingers were too thick to grip
the brush right. The sky was always green
and hay spoiled in the fields. In wind,
the rain, the superlative night, images came, geese

skimming to the reservoir. This old man listened.
He got a bigger brush and once painted the cry
of a goose so long, it floated off the canvas
into thin air. Things got better. Sky turned white.
Winter came and he became quite expert at snowflakes.
But he was growing wise, Lord, his hair white as snow.

Funny, he used to say, how mountains are blue
in winter and green in spring. He never ever
got things quite right. He thought a lot about the day
the goose bit Grandma's hand. LIFE seldom came
the shade he wanted. Well, and yes, he died well,
but you should have seen how well his friends took it.

Ouch,

Gravely

we watched her go the way she came,
unenvied, wild—cold as last spring rain.
Mule deer browsed her garden down
to labored earth, seed and clean carrots.

Dusk is never easy, yet she took it
like her plastic saint, grandly, the day
we cut those morning glories down
and divvied up her odds and ends.

Daughters burned sheets the following Monday.
All over God's city, the high white stars
welcomed her the way she'd planned: a chilly
satellite ringing round the great malicious moon.

Grandfather at the Rest Home

I am standing high and frail.
Worms are breathing in my bones.
My eyes are cataracts
and dams back up my blood.
The birds are singing chirps,
chirps go in my ears.
I am drowning.

I should have known you would come
today, the birds sing
in my bones. Stranger to me now,
your words go through the grass
like snakes. My appetite is pure
for the quick sweet taste of apples.

Apples, here come the apples.
That bulgy, baggy brown sack
you carry in your skin
is filled with apples.

Apples for me now,
apples for the king!

Oh, that murderous, knifing waltz
we counted on so many years ago
is going, gone, the price the keen apples.
My blood sings the birds farewell.

Ouch.

Legends Like This

Here it is written: Stoned
before the cross, three dark poets
dying in the sight of God.

He gave them everything:
eyes, teeth, heart,
their beautiful bones.

He never learned their names.
Oh, they tried everything:
they knelt, they sprawled

face down upon the altar,
killed their beautiful parents.
He never thought to tell them

what He wanted, who they were . . .
and they, of course, burned His church
and hid out for a long, long time.

Lady in a Distant Face

The odd way you comb your hair,
those big hands drawing circles in a room
and a Mormon background—you become
the Sunday all-day Scotch friend
that needs a friend to keep these mountains back.

We came upcountry, not knowing
your Paris days, the summer-wide search
for Frenchmen with wild hair
and eyes that made for easy lies.
No life is chilly as your own
when time makes parents foreign and brothers
come to mock you when you're drunk.

Summer was no lifetime. It rolled with games
and play on sand with sullen kings.
Bikinis fit you then; you fit the beaches
with your famous boys—life so shallow
you could end it with a kiss.

What bird could go alone this unnoticed?
On those beaches—did you fly for seven years,
then drop, exhausted, in the sea?
The fishermen—they knew you for a fraud,
rescued you with words that meant go home.

Home. The steamer edged you
from that scene of what is nice, the Paris days
of sun and mortgaged gold.
And now, here, in these mountains
that hold you from yourself, the wind
blowing down your final face,
you tell us what we know: Time is clean
and brief for girls in a wild time,
past for ladies up like smoke in narrow wind.

Never Give a Bum an Even Break

He could have come to tell us
of his new-found luck—the strolling
players who offered him a role
in their latest comedy, or the uncle
who promised him hundreds of dollars
just to stay away—instead he spoke
of a role so black the uncle died
out of luck in a west-end shack.
I walked him to the door. Behind me
my house, my wife and mirror disappeared.

We sit now, a steady demolition team,
under one of the oldest bridges in town.
Any day we will crawl out to settle
old scores or create new roles, our masks
glittering in a comic rain.

Acknowledgments

The following poems have been published previously in the following books and periodicals, and where indicated, the author and publisher wish to acknowledge permission to reprint:

"Two for the Festival," "Never Give a Bum an Even Break," "Riding the Earthboy 40," "The Last Priest Didn't Even Say Goodbye," and "Getting Things Straight" in *Hearse*; "Blue Like Death" in *Inscape*; "The Renegade Wants Words" in *Kayak*; "D-Y Bar" and "Spring for all Seasons" in *The Malahat Review*; "In My First Hard Springtime" and "Christmas Comes to Moccasin Flat" in *Poetry Northwest*; "Lady in a Distant Face," "The Day to Make Up Incompletes," "Song for the Season" in *Sumac*; "Visit," "You Gone, the King Dead," "Day After Chasing Porcupines" in *Unicorn Journal*; "Dancing Man" in *Harper's Bazaar*; "Christmas Comes to Moccasin Flat" in *Since Feeling Is First*, published by Scott, Foresman, and Company; "Snow Country Weavers" and "Surviving" first appeared in the *South Dakota Review*, Summer, 1969, and are reprinted with permission of the editor, John R. Milton; "Harlem, Montana: Just Off the Reservation" and "Dreaming Winter" in *Poetry*; "The Versatile Historian," "In My Lifetime," and "There are Silent Legends" in *New American Review*; "Plea to Those Who Matter" and "Going to Remake This World" are from *Intro # 1*, edited by R. V. Cassill. Copyright 1968 by Bantam Books, Inc; the poem "The Only Bar in Dixon" appeared originally in *The New Yorker*.

Vincent Bourdon

James Welch (1940–2003) was the author of five novels, including *Fools Crow*, which won the American Book Award, the *Los Angeles Times Book Award*, and the Pacific Northwest Booksellers Award, and one work of nonfiction, *Killing Custer*. He attended schools on the Blackfeet and Fort Belknap reservations in Montana and studied writing at the University of Montana under the legendary writing teacher Richard Hugo.

James Tate was born in Kansas City, Missouri, in 1943. He is the author of numerous books of poetry, including *Worshipful Company of Fletchers* (1994), which won the National Book Award, and *Selected Poems* (1991), which won the Pulitzer Prize. He was also the recipient of the 1995 Wallace Stevens Award from the Academy of American Poets. He teaches at the University of Massachusetts in Amherst.

Penguin Poets

Ted Berrigan
Selected Poems
The Sonnets

Philip Booth
Lifelines

Jim Carroll
Fear of Dreaming
Void of Course

Carl Dennis
New and Selected Poems 1974–2004
Practical Gods

Barbara Cully
Desire Reclining

Diane di Prima
Loba

Stuart Dischell
Dig Safe

Stephen Dobyns
Pallbearers Envying the One Who Rides
The Porcupine's Kisses

Roger Fanning
Homesick

Amy Gerstler
Crown of Weeds
Ghost Girl
Medicine
Nerve Storm

Debora Greger
Desert Fathers, Uranium Daughters
God
Western Art

Robert Hunter
Sentinel

Barbara Jordan
Trace Elements

Mary Karr
Viper Rum

Jack Kerouac
Book of Blues
Book of Haikus

Joanne Kyger
As Ever

Ann Lauterbach
If in Time
On a Stair

Phyllis Levin
Mercury

William Logan
Macbeth in Venice
Night Battle
Vain Empires

Derek Mahon
Selected Poems

Michael McClure
Huge Dreams: San Francisco and Beat Poems

Carol Muske
An Octave Above Thunder

Alice Notley
The Descent of Alette
Disobedience
Mysteries of Small Houses

Lawrence Raab
The Probable World
Visible Signs

Pattiann Rogers
Generations

Stephanie Strickland
V

Anne Waldman
Kill or Cure
Marriage: A Sentence
Structure of the World Compared to a Bubble

James Welch
Riding the Earthboy 40

Philip Whalen
Overtime: Selected Poems

Robert Wrigley
Lives of the Animals
Reign of Snakes

John Yau
Borrowed Love Poems